DEC   2006

DU

DIAMONDS
AND OTHER GEMS

NEIL MORRIS

DUFFIELD BRANCH LIBRARY
2507 W. GRAND BLVD.
DETROIT, MI 48208-1236
(313) 224-6456

043637620

A+

Smart Apple Media

Published by Smart Apple Media
2140 Howard Drive West
North Mankato, MN 56003

Design and production by Guy Callaby

Photographs by Corbis (Archivo Iconografico
S.A., D. AUBERT / CORBIS SYGMA, Morton
Beebe, BISSON BERNARD / CORBIS SYGMA,
Richard Bickel, The Cover Story, VO TRUNG
DUNG / CORBIS SYGMA, Michael Freeman,
Roger Garwood & Trish Ainslie, Rick Gayle, Lowell
Georgia, Mark E. Gibson, COLLART HERVE /
CORBIS SYGMA, Historical Picture Archive, Ann
Johansson, Peter Johnson, Thom Lang, Danny
Lehman, Charles & Josette Lenars, Chris Lisle,
PETER MACDIARMID / Reuters, Ludovic Maisant,
Francis G. Mayer, Stephanie Maze, Richard T.
Nowitz, Charles O'Rear, Gianni Dagli Orti, Christine
Osborne, Reuters, Philip Richardson; Gallo Images),
Getty Images (Jody Dole), Photo Researchers, Inc.
(David Parker), Photri

Copyright © 2006 Smart Apple Media.
International copyright reserved in all countries.
No part of this book may be reproduced in any
form without written permission from the publisher.

Printed in Thailand

Library of Congress Cataloging-in-Publication Data

Morris, Neil, 1946–
Diamonds and other gems / by Neil Morris.
p. cm. — (Earth's resources)
Includes index.
ISBN 1-58340-629-8
1. Diamonds—Juvenile literature. 2. Precious
stones—Juvenile literature. I. Title.

QE393.M67 2005
553.8'2—dc22   2004056487

First Edition

9 8 7 6 5 4 3 2 1

CONTENTS

INTRODUCTION

Gemstones are found in some of the rocks that make up Earth's surface. The planet's rocks are made of solid chemical substances called minerals, and we call those that are especially beautiful and rare gemstones.

In their natural state, most gemstones have a rough texture and an irregular shape. To bring out the stones' beauty, experts cut and polish them into gems or jewels. Fewer than 100 of more than 2,000 different minerals are considered gemstones. Some of the most famous are also known as precious stones. These include diamonds, rubies, sapphires, and emeralds. Others, such as amethyst and garnet, are sometimes called semiprecious stones. Of all the gems, diamonds are considered the most beautiful, and they are certainly the most valuable.

This is how rough, uncut diamonds look just after they have been extracted from ore.

Prehistoric carbon

Diamond is made of pure carbon and is the hardest naturally occurring substance in the world. The word "diamond" comes from the Greek word *adamas*, which means "unconquerable." It was given the name because it cannot be scratched or dented by other substances. The other main form of the element carbon is graphite, which is very different from diamond because it is soft. Some diamonds were formed more than three billion years ago, which makes them two-thirds as old as Earth itself. Diamond crystals sometimes form cubes, but most often they are found as eight-sided shapes.

Color and sparkle

While some of the most valuable diamonds are colorless, other gemstones are known for their brilliant, pure colors. Different shades have become associated with certain gems, such as ruby red, emerald green, sapphire blue, and amethyst purple. Individual stones sometimes show different colors because of their slightly different structure, but they all sparkle as light passes through them. Cut diamonds are known as "sparklers" because they are the most brilliant. Some gems also show flashes of rainbow colors when they are turned in the light. Jewelers call this flashing feature "fire."

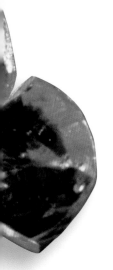

These diamonds have been cut and polished. They may have lost up to half their weight during these processes, but they have grown enormously in value.

This group of zircon gems shows a range of colors, including red, blue, and green. Sometimes the colors are produced artificially by heating brown stones. Some colorless zircons have such sparkle that they may be mistaken for diamonds.

More than three-quarters of the world's emeralds come from Colombia, in South America. Here, Colombian jewelers are hard at work.

Diamonds have been discovered in most parts of the world. They are mined in about 25 countries and on every continent except Europe and Antarctica.

The leading producers of rough diamonds are Australia, Botswana, and Russia. Between them, these three countries produce almost two-thirds of the world's diamonds. They are followed by two more African countries: Democratic Republic of Congo and South Africa. Mining and production increased dramatically all over the world during the 20th century, from the hot deserts of Africa and Australia to the cold, frozen wilderness of northern Canada and Russian Siberia. The range of other gems is also a worldwide resource, with some countries specializing in certain varieties. Experts believe that the best rubies come from Myanmar, for example, and the best topaz from Brazil.

Beneath the desert sands

The Republic of Botswana, in southern Africa, became an independent country in 1966. The following year, diamonds were discovered and a mine was opened near the town of Orapa. A few years later, another mine opened in the southeastern region of the Kalahari Desert. This mine, at Jwaneng, is still very productive today, and experts have estimated that the region's existing mines will continue producing diamonds for at least 40 years. Botswanan diamonds are of high quality, and three-quarters of them are used as jewels. Other gemstones are also mined in Botswana, as well as the precious metal gold.

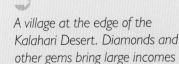

A village at the edge of the Kalahari Desert. Diamonds and other gems bring large incomes to many African countries.

The old port of Antwerp, where conferences and trade fairs are regularly held in the diamond district. The city also has the Diamond Museum.

Diamond-trading center

The largest city in Belgium, Antwerp, is the world's biggest and most important diamond-trading center. The city took this title from Venice, Paris, and other centers of trade in the 16th century. Today, Antwerp has its own diamond district, and more than three-quarters of the world's uncut diamonds pass through the city. About 18,000 people work in the industry, which expanded in Belgium when a flood of rough diamonds came onto the market from South Africa in the 19th century. The world's other great gem-trading centers are Bombay, Tel Aviv, New York, and London.

MINERAL PROPERTIES

Mineralogists—people who study minerals—identify and classify gemstones according to their properties, or characteristic features. These include the shape of their crystals and one of the most obvious qualities: color.

Hardness is also important, as is the way in which a gemstone breaks or splits, which is called its cleavage. Most gemstones split cleanly along lines of weakness to make a flat surface, but sometimes they leave an uneven fracture. Diamonds are often cut along their lines of cleavage. Gemstones also bend light as it passes through them, which gives them their flashing brilliance. Some gems separate white light into different colors. All of these different properties can be measured by experts.

Experts, such as this gemologist in Russia, check the properties of individual gemstones. They use special instruments to see how much the stones bend light.

Crystal structure

Like other minerals, gemstones have a crystal structure. This means that the atoms of which they are made line up in a regular, geometric arrangement. Crystals have a definite pattern that is always the same, so they form special shapes. Mineralogists call these shapes "crystal habits." Diamonds and garnets are said to form cubic crystals, but a diamond's most common shape is the eight-faced octahedron. Other gems have different crystal habits. For example, emeralds and aquamarines are generally hexagonal, or six-sided.

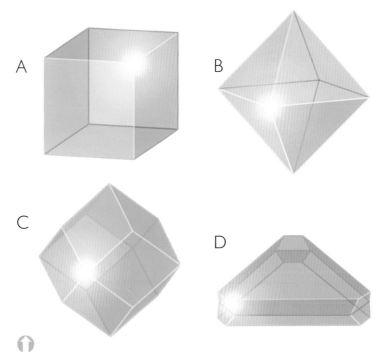

Some of the most common diamond crystal shapes: A) simple cube; B) octahedron; C) dodecahedron; D) twinned macle.

An expert studies a large ruby. As a form of corundum, this is one of the hardest stones.

Hardness

A gemstone's hardness can be measured by its ability to scratch a mark on another mineral. All gemstones can be given a number according to the Mohs scale of hardness, which lists 10 minerals from 1 to 10. Talc is the softest mineral, and diamond is the hardest. Near the top of the scale, the minerals get very hard. Diamond is four times harder than corundum, which is itself four times as hard as quartz.

Mohs Number	Mineral	Equivalent
1	talc	baby powder
2	gypsum	fingernail
3	calcite	copper coin
4	fluorite	iron nail
5	apatite	knife blade
6	feldspar	glass
7	quartz	steel file
8	topaz	sandpaper
9	corundum	none
10	diamond	none

MINING

Most diamonds are found in a kind of rock called kimberlite, which was first found in South Africa and forms vertical pipes from underground to the surface. In 1979, another kind of diamond rock, called lamproite, was discovered in Australia. The rocks can be recovered from so-called opencast or open-pit mines near the surface, or shafts can be dug underground.

The same is true for other gemstones, which are found in different kinds of rock. In many places, huge amounts of rock have to be mined in order to recover a very small number of gems. Sometimes diamonds and other gemstones can also be found in gravel, especially on the beds of rivers, lakes, and seas. This happens where the gem-bearing rocks have been worn away by the weather at Earth's surface.

The Big Hole, near the city of Kimberley in South Africa, which gave its name to the rock kimberlite. Diamonds were mined underground to a depth of 3,600 feet (1,100 m), and the hole itself is 700 feet (215 m) deep. Today there is a museum beside the old mine.

Tunneling underground

For underground diamond-mining, vertical shafts are dug down from the surface. Horizontal tunnels then lead off the shafts to the pipes that contain diamond-bearing ore deposits. Miners used to operate drills to remove chunks of ore from the rock face, but today much of this work is done by remote-controlled, electric drilling equipment. This is a difficult operation, because the rocks must be removed and then crushed and screened without damaging the diamonds. After any large diamonds have been taken out and the ore has been reduced to gravel, it is passed across a sloping steel table that is covered with grease. Diamonds stick to grease, so they can then be picked out by sorters.

This processing plant stands beside the Finsch diamond mine, 100 miles (160 km) from Kimberley, in South Africa. It has both an open pit and underground tunnels.

Open pits

Opencast diamond mines are dug in a series of horizontal layers called benches, and roads connect them to the surface level. The mines are often very wide and deep. Emeralds and other gemstones are mined in the same way. In Colombia, there is an area known as the "emerald rectangle," where there are several large opencast mines. Once benches have been made, the exposed rock is carefully inspected by workers using simple hand tools.

The Argyle diamond mine, in western Australia, was first dug in 1985. In a typical year, miners remove about 11 million tons (10 million t) of ore, which produce about 6.5 tons (6 t) of diamonds. Argyle has become famous for its pink diamonds.

CUTTING AND POLISHING

Rough gemstones are cut and polished before being sold for use in jewelry. The art of doing this is known as lapidary, and the person who does the work is also called a lapidary.

First, an expert looks at each particular stone for imperfections and direction of cleavage. Then he or she marks the stone to show how it should be cut. The stone may be sawed into two or more pieces using a diamond-tipped, rotating disk that acts as a blade. Some stones are then shaped into a cabochon, which has a rounded, dome shape and a flat base. Others are cut with a number of flat, polished faces called facets. This is done by holding the stone against a revolving disk that has a top layer of diamond dust. The facets are carefully created so that they reflect light and show the gemstone at its beautiful best.

A lapidary at work. This is a highly skilled profession, and there are many amateur clubs for people who are interested in taking up lapidary as a hobby.

The four c's

Polished gems are graded according to features known as the "four c's": their carats (units of weight), clarity, color, and cut. One carat equals 200 milligrams and is divided into 100 points. This scale has nothing to do with the carats that measure the purity of precious metals. The higher the carat, the more valuable the gemstone. A gem's clarity might be affected by small marks, cracks, or bubbles, which would reduce its value. Color depends on the particular stone; in the case of diamonds, many people consider colorless stones to be the best. The cut is the shape made by a lapidary.

Gem factories

Many top-quality gemstones are cut and polished in Antwerp, Belgium. But in recent years, much of this work has gone to India. Surat, an industrial port in the state of Gujarat, has become the center of India's successful diamond-polishing industry, where many thousands of cutters work in gem factories. Like many gem miners, the lapidaries are watched over by closed-circuit cameras to make sure that none of the rough or polished diamonds disappear.

The brilliant cut is one of the most famous cuts for diamonds. It is made up of 58 facets and reflects light to the best effect. It is also used on rubies, sapphires, and emeralds.

A gem-cutter at work in Jaipur, India. The city is famous for jewelry.

Deposits of diamonds and other gemstones were found around the Hyderabad region of India in ancient times. They were bought and sold in the city of Golconda, and the earliest written mention of diamonds is in a Sanskrit manuscript dating from about 300 B.C.

Historians believe that gemstones were kept as talismans, which were thought to protect their owners and give them magical powers. Later, gems were taken up by rulers and leaders as symbols of power and authority. In the 13th century, French King Louis IX decided that diamonds could be worn only by the monarch. During the following century, the earliest gem-cutting took place in Venice. India remained the world's main source of supply until diamonds were found in Brazil in the 18th century.

This portrait of Catherine the Great (1729–96), empress of Russia, shows her wearing royal jewels and pearls.

Star of Africa

In 1905, an enormous diamond was found in a South African mine. Weighing 3,106 carats (21.7 ounces, or 621 g) and named the *Cullinan*, it was presented to King Edward VII of Great Britain. This magnificent stone was cut into 9 large gems and 96 smaller ones. The *Cullinan's* largest cut diamond was the 530-carat (3.7 ounces, or 106 g) *Star of Africa*, which now forms part of the British Crown Jewels. Another famous diamond, called the *Koh-i-noor* (or "Mountain of Light"), was presented to Queen Victoria and set in a crown made in 1937 for Queen Elizabeth the Queen Mother. According to legend, any woman possessing it will rule the world.

 The Royal Scepter is a rod of gold, with the Star of Africa held in a heart-shaped mount. Above this is an amethyst with a diamond-encrusted cross set with an emerald.

Portuguese officials watch Brazilians washing diamonds.

Two great finds

In 1725, miners panning for gold found diamonds in Brazil, which then belonged to Portugal. For the next 150 years, Brazil was the world's leading source of diamonds. The next great find was in South Africa, which today produces 15 times more diamonds than Brazil. In 1867, a 15-year-old boy playing on the banks of the Orange River near his father's farm found a transparent stone that turned out to be South Africa's first known diamond. This led to a diamond rush in the region and the discovery of the Kimberley gem fields.

CORUNDUM

Pure corundum is a very hard, colorless mineral with the chemical name aluminum oxide. Small amounts of impurities in the mineral give it different colors, and these make two very famous gemstones. Red corundum, given its rich color by traces of the metal chromium, is called ruby (from the Latin word for "red").

All other varieties, and especially the blue corundum caused by traces of iron and titanium, are called sapphire (from the Greek word for "blue stone"). There are also pink, yellow, and orange sapphires. Some varieties of corundum are mined from the marble and other rocks in which they formed, but most are found in river gravel near their original source. They are found in many different parts of the world.

Gem merchants selling uncut corundum stones, which will be weighed accurately on the scales.

Mogok Stone Tract

Some of the world's best rubies are found in the so-called Mogok Stone Tract, north of Mandalay in Myanmar (formerly called Burma). The hilly region around the town of Mogok is made up of marble, schist, gneiss, granite, and limestone rocks, and rubies and sapphires have been mined here for hundreds of years. At many of the mines, pits or trenches are dug into the hillside, and the rocks are carefully broken up to find the gemstones. The most famous rubies from the region have a glowing red color that is known locally as "pigeon's blood."

Mining for rubies near Mogok, in Myanmar. The region, called a "stone tract" by geologists, is also known as the Valley of Rubies.

Starry effect

Some rubies and sapphires reflect light in a six-rayed star pattern. This is caused by needle-shaped crystals of the mineral rutile in the gemstone, and gemologists call the effect asterism. The star shape is shown best when the gem is polished in a cabochon shape. The *Star of India* is the largest star sapphire in the world. It weighs 563 carats (3.9 ounces, or 113 g) and was found in Sri Lanka in the 17th century. It was presented to the American Museum of Natural History in New York in 1900, and it is still a popular exhibit today.

A beautiful selection of blood-red rubies.

BERYL

Like corundum, pure beryl is a colorless mineral.
Its chemical name is beryllium aluminum silicate,
and it has two famous forms with different colors.
Rich green beryl has traces of chromium and is called
emerald, while traces of iron help form greenish-blue
aquamarine (which means "seawater" and is
a reference to its color).

There are two other, less well-known kinds of beryl: golden-yellow heliodor (sometimes called golden beryl) and pink morganite (named in 1911 after an American banker, John Pierpoint Morgan). All of the different forms of beryl score 7.5 on the Mohs scale of hardness (see page 9), which places them between quartz and topaz. This is hard enough to make a very durable range of gems.

A Brazilian master jeweler examines aquamarines in his office in Rio de Janeiro.

Colombian emeralds

The world's best emeralds are found in Colombia. When Spanish conquistadors arrived there in the 16th century, they discovered that Native American groups such as the Chibcha and Muzo had been mining and trading emeralds for many centuries. However, they did not give up their mining secrets easily. They also deceived the Europeans by saying that real emeralds would not shatter when hit with a hammer. This is untrue, since most emeralds are flawed and fractured, and the Spaniards destroyed many gems believing they were worthless. Today, individual Colombian mines give their names to different varieties of emeralds, which are found in shale and limestone rocks. Chivor emeralds have a warm, grassy-green color with a yellowish tinge, while Muzo emeralds are a deeper, bluish green.

This handful of small emeralds comes from Colombia's famous Muzo mine.

Workers at the Santa Maria de Itabira mine in Brazil, one of the world's best sources of top-quality aquamarine.

Brazilian aquamarines

South America—especially its largest country, Brazil—is also the best source for aquamarines. One of the most famous Brazilian mines, Santa Maria de Itabira, has given its name to a deep blue aquamarine. This is known throughout the world as "Santa Maria," and similar gemstones found in Mozambique, Namibia, and other African countries are referred to as "Santa Maria Africana." Africa may have been a source of aquamarine for the ancient Romans, who believed that carrying it made their soldiers more courageous.

A RANGE OF COLORS

Most gem minerals, such as ruby, emerald, and amethyst, show color as light passes through them. Some, such as opal, come in a wide range of colors. This gem's name comes from the Sanskrit word upala, meaning "precious stone," and it was greatly prized in ancient times.

Precious opals show a play of color that is seen as flashes of all the colors of the rainbow. Yet the main color of the stone varies, and black opals are considered the most valuable. Other minerals, such as turquoise, jade, and lapis lazuli, are almost opaque, which means light cannot be seen through them. Nevertheless, they are popular for their beautiful colors, as well as their interesting textures and patterns.

Opal forms in small cavities in rocks. These Australian fire opals show the shape of shells that were once buried in rocks.

Hard and soft jade

The precious stone that we call jade was very popular in ancient China for carving into jewelry and burying with the dead. Later, it was used in a similar way by the Maya and other people of Central America. In 1863, French mineralogist Alexis Damour discovered that the name jade was being used for two different minerals. The first, called jadeite or sometimes "hard jade," measures up to 7 on the Mohs hardness scale (the same as quartz). The second, nephrite or "soft jade," measures 6.5 and was known to the ancient Chinese as the "stone of the heavens." Both minerals were originally used in weapons and tools, and then later for delicate carvings. The most prized variety has always been "imperial jade," which has an emerald-green color.

This jadeite mask was made by the ancient Olmec people of Mexico more than 2,000 years ago.

Varieties of quartz

Quartz is a name for silica or silicon dioxide. The purest form of this mineral is colorless, transparent rock crystal. But as with other gemstones, colored varieties are created by chemical impurities. Traces of iron are found in the two most famous varieties: violet or purple amethyst and yellow citrine. The color can be changed by heating, and a lot of so-called citrine is made commercially by heating amethyst. Crystals of amethyst are often found inside a hollow rock mass called a geode, and these can form beautiful ornaments in their natural state.

These amethyst crystals line a geode.

JEWELRY

Along with precious metals, gemstones have been used in jewelry since ancient times. Seen by kings and queens as a sign of wealth and power, they were used to adorn crowns and other royal regalia. English King Henry VIII (1491–1547) probably possessed more jewelry than his six wives. He is thought to have had more than 200 rings and 300 brooches.

Later, women wore much more jewelry than men, and diamonds, emeralds, rubies, and other gems became the most popular items for rings, necklaces, and bracelets. Today, fine individual pieces are still made by jewelry designers. Genuine gemstones are very expensive, so designs are often imitated by shopping mall stores as costume jewelry made with colored glass. Most valuable historical pieces are now in museums.

This portrait of Henry VIII, painted in 1536, shows his great love of jewelry. It includes an elaborate pendant necklace. The painter, Hans Holbein the Younger, designed some of the king's jewelry.

A diamond is forever

In 1477, Archduke Maximilian of Austria gave a diamond ring to his future wife, Mary of Burgundy. This may have started the tradition of diamond engagement rings, which still continues today. In 1948, an advertising copywriter in New York invented the famous slogan, "A diamond is forever." Since then, diamond rings have become even more popular, and most people consider all forms of diamond jewelry to be the best. The famous steel-blue *Hope Diamond* was found in India in the 16th century and was owned by kings of France before being bought by English banker Henry Hope in 1830. Once part of a medallion, it was made the centerpiece of a diamond necklace by jeweler Pierre Cartier and given to an American museum in 1958.

The Hope Diamond *(the large central stone) was once known to French royalty as the "Blue Diamond of the Crown." It weighs 45.52 carats (one-third of an ounce, or 9.1 g).*

This Egyptian pectoral was found in Tutankhamen's tomb. Taking the shape of a sacred scarab beetle, it is set with red carnelian, green feldspar, blue lapis lazuli, and turquoise.

Ancient Egyptian gems

The ancient Egyptians made and wore jewelry from the earliest times. Their jewelry was particularly beautiful during the Middle Kingdom (2055–1650 B.C.), when many different kinds of gemstones were used to decorate diadems, pendants, bracelets, and rings. The Egyptians believed that gems had magical powers and wore them for good luck as well as adornment. Many items were placed in tombs, especially those of queens and princesses, for use in the afterlife. The famous finds at Tutankhamen's tomb in the Valley of the Kings included fabulous jewelry.

BIRTHSTONES AND BELIEFS

There are many different traditions associated with gemstones, including the belief that each month of the year has its own stone. Each gem is supposed to have its own meaning, especially for a person born in that month.

In the first century A.D., Jewish historian Flavius Josephus linked these beliefs to the breastplate worn by the high priest, as described in the Old Testament of the Bible. The breastplate had four rows of three gemstones to represent the Twelve Tribes of Israel. In more recent times, people came to think that wearing their birthstone would bring them luck. But the opposite could be true, too. There is a superstition that it is very bad luck for those not born in October to wear opal, for example.

The birthstones are:

This 19th-century lithograph shows the high priest Eli, wearing a gemstone breastplate, with his young assistant Samuel. In the Bible, the stones are listed as sardius (ruby), topaz, carbuncle (garnet), emerald, sapphire, diamond, ligure (zircon), agate, amethyst, beryl (aquamarine), onyx, and jasper.

Month	Gemstone	Meaning
January	garnet	faithfulness
February	amethyst	sincerity
March	aquamarine	courage
April	diamond	innocence
May	emerald	love
June	alexandrite	health
July	ruby	happiness
August	sardonyx	satisfaction
September	sapphire	clear thinking
October	opal	hope
November	topaz	loyalty
December	turquoise	prosperity

Garnet

The birthstone for January is actually the name of a group of similar minerals. Most garnets are red in color, although there is a vivid green variety. The ancient Greeks called garnet the "lamp stone" and believed that wearing it helped people see in the dark, and an old legend states that dragons' eyes were made of garnet. The gem was also thought to be useful in stopping a wound from bleeding. By the 13th century, garnet jewels were being worn to ward off evil spirits (and insects!).

These brownish-red garnets come from Madagascar.

Health and happiness

Today, some people believe that gemstones have special healing powers. Many books have been written about "crystal healing" and "gemstone therapy." The belief is that different kinds of gems have their own energy, and that people can tap into this and benefit from it by wearing the gems, or by touching or gazing at them. For example, diamonds are supposed to help people think clearly and be more determined, rubies help them overcome fear, and jade can help people relax.

Some people buy precious stones for their healing properties as well as their beauty.

USEFUL RESOURCES

Out of every five diamonds mined, only one is normally good enough to be used as a gem. The others are used in industry, where they are valuable because of their hardness and other properties. Because they are so hard, diamonds, rubies, and sapphires are used to test the hardness of other materials and to shape them.

Diamonds are also used in an instrument called a diamond-anvil pressure cell, which can apply greater forces and higher pressures on other objects than any other machine. This is very useful to research scientists and has increased our understanding of the enormous pressures that exist at the center of Earth. Before laser technology and CD players developed, diamond-tipped needles were used to play vinyl records. Today, diamonds are even used as transparent windows for certain optical devices, for example in spacecraft.

Researchers are working on putting small amounts of powdered diamond into car paints, making them tougher and longer-lasting.

Drills and cutters

Diamonds are so hard that they can be used to cut, drill and grind all kinds of metals and other materials. Rough diamonds can be set into cutting tools, or they may be crushed before being put on the edges of cutting tools using great heat. Grains of gray, opaque diamonds are used to make bort, which in turn is used to make grinding wheels and drill bits. Even darker industrial diamonds make up carbonado, which is used in making rock-cutting saws and glass-cutters.

This drill bit has industrial diamonds set into its face. It will cut into anything!

You can see the tiny jewels in the mechanism of this watch.

Watch jewels

Jewels are often used as bearings in mechanical watches and clocks. Because their surface is smooth and hard, they allow axles, gears, and pivots to turn freely, and they last longer than other materials. The jewels are usually rubies, sapphires, garnets, or diamonds. Today, the most common watch jewels are highly polished synthetic rubies or sapphires. Most high-quality watches made before 1900 had up to 15 jewels, but during the 20th century, this number grew to as many as 100. Some jewels may have been put in simply to increase the value of the timepiece.

TODAY AND TOMORROW

Diamonds and all kinds of other gems are as popular as ever, and some countries are increasing their production from mines each year. In some parts of the world, mining and industrial processes are having a big impact on the environment, and governments and environmentalists are trying to make sure that gem-mining does not damage local communities.

At the same time, lasers and other equipment are increasingly used to improve the quality of gems by removing tiny faults. Also, more synthetic gems are being produced, especially for use in industry. All of this means that we humans have more control over the creation of gems, but it is still the genuine, natural article that most appeals to people all over the world.

This Indian bride wears jewels and pearls for her Hindu wedding. As in many other parts of the world, diamonds are seen as symbols of love in India.

Synthetics

Around 50 years ago, scientists realized that they could make diamonds from graphite (the other form of carbon). They did this by applying enormous pressure and tremendous heat to the mineral, eventually producing industrial-quality diamonds. Since then, companies have learned to make jewel-quality diamonds and other gems. Rubies and sapphires are made by heating aluminum oxide in a special way. It is likely that future technology will continue to improve the quality of synthetic gems, making them more difficult to distinguish from natural gems.

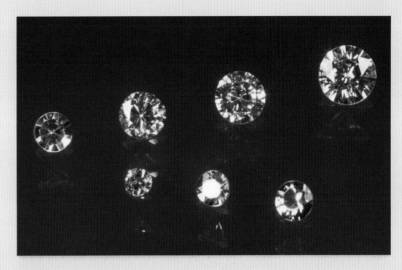

 These synthetic diamonds have been cut in the same way as natural gems.

Conflict diamonds

In recent years, diamonds have been used to pay for guns and fund civil wars and other conflicts in African countries such as Sierra Leone, Angola, Democratic Republic of Congo, Central African Republic, and Liberia. Paying in so-called "conflict diamonds" has helped terrorists and other groups avoid the normal banking system. A new system of controls, using computer databases and certificates, has been set up to try to stop this illegal trade by tracking diamonds and making governments, traders, and gem buyers more aware of the problem.

 Loss of traditional lands is a problem in Africa. In 2004, representatives of the Bushmen people of Botswana demonstrated in London against being moved from their ancestral homeland to make way for diamond mines.

GLOSSARY

asterism A star-shape effect that can be seen in some gemstones.

bench A horizontal layer or flat ledge in an opencast mine.

bort Diamond grains used in cutting, grinding, and drilling tools.

brilliant cut A special cut for diamonds and other gems with 58 facets.

cabochon A rounded, dome shape with a flat base; also, a gem with this shape.

carat A unit of weight used for gemstones (1 carat = 200 mg).

carbonado Dark diamonds used in cutting, grinding, and drilling tools.

cleavage The splitting of minerals, especially along lines of weakness.

continent One of Earth's seven huge land masses.

costume jewelry Jewelry made with imitation gems such as colored glass.

crystal A solid form of mineral with a regular, geometrical shape.

dodecahedron A 12-faced shape.

element A substance that cannot be separated into a simpler form.

environmentalist A person who is concerned about and acts to protect the natural environment.

extract To take out or obtain something from a source.

facet One of the faces of a cut gemstone.

fracture Break.

gemologist A scientist who studies gemstones.

geode A hollow mass of rock with crystals inside.

gravel A deposit of loose stones and other fragments.

lapidary The art of cutting and polishing gemstones; also, a skilled person who does this work.

macle A crystal that is twinned (made up of a pair of crystals).

mineral A solid chemical substance that occurs naturally in the earth.

mineralogist A scientist who studies and classifies minerals.

octahedron An eight-faced shape.

opaque Describing something that cannot be seen through.

opencast or **open-pit mine** A mine in which ore is extracted at or near Earth's surface.

ore Rock or mineral containing a useful metal or valuable mineral.

precious metal One of the valuable metals—gold, silver, or platinum.

property A characteristic feature (of a mineral).

refractive index Measurement of the speed of light as it passes through and is bent by different substances such as minerals.

refractometer An instrument that measures the refractive index of minerals.

rough diamond An uncut diamond.

synthetic Made artificially by a chemical process.

talisman A stone or jewel that is thought to protect and give magical power to its wearer.

tract An area of land.

transparent See-through.

INDEX